CLEANING UP AFTER

THE PARTIES

THE HIGH COST OF PARTY POLITICS

They Promised Us the Moon
Volume II

BY

WILLIAM PARKER ARCHIBALD

CLEANING UP AFTER THE PARTIES
They Promised Us the Moon– Volume II

Textual Advisement: Elaine Bush
Technical Support: Digital Depot (Maurice Tift)
Editing: Kit Duncan
Book Layout: Nat Mara

*A writer should struggle with the words
so the reader won't have to.*

– the author

When I was a youngster,

My father's favorite joke was about the farmer who had a pig with a wooden leg. When asked about it, the farmer went on for days about the virtues of the pig and how attached the family had become to it.

Acknowledging all of that, the visitor asked yet again why the animal had a wooden leg. To which the farmer responded, "Well, if you had a pig like that, would you eat it all at once?"

This, in a real way, is the story of America. I'm not questioning our love for it. That is well established. Rather, I'm questioning why, after centuries of toil and sacrifice, we've all of a sudden turned on it and are now devouring it with the reckless abandon of fools who sat down to feast on the goose that laid the golden egg.

Dedication

This book, indeed this whole endeavor to preserve, protect and defend that which has been given to us at such enormous cost, is dedicated to all of the patriots, both living and dead and to my good friend and mentor,

Millard Fuller,
founder of Habitat for Humanity International and the Fuller Center for Housing.

CLEANING

UP

AFTER THE

PARTIES

The Great American
Tune-up

Feeling Invisible

Unlike newly formed democracies where people walk miles and miles in order to cast their vote and get that coveted splash of ink on their finger, we feel so powerless, so unable to be heard in this country that many of us have intentionally tuned out.

I see it all of the time. I ask people, particularly younger people, about what's going on out there in the world around them and find an astonishingly high percentage don't have the slightest clue. When I pepper them with questions, it becomes readily apparent that they don't read the paper or watch the news and neither do any of the people in their home. That sense of wanting, of needing to know because "I want to cast my vote or write my Congressman or fight for this or that cause" is all but completely gone.

This is what lobbyists, special interests, big money and pollsters that broadcast what people are thinking long before they even think it have done to this country. Gone is the sense that we have something to contribute, that our perspective is worthy of notice, that our voices and letters to Congress have an impact. I, for one, know of nothing sadder. For in this listless, thoughtless malaise we find the termites of apathy eating away at the pillars of this grand old house, this marvel of American poplar and oak, pine and maple, hewn by the sweat of patriots all. The visuals remain. They are still intact, but the trouble lies beneath the surface, for the core has been hollowed out, leaving the entire structure strained and weakened.

Fair Warning

People wrongly assume that by doing nothing, things will remain largely unchanged. Obviously, these people have never had much experience with termites. If they had, they'd realize that every day that these tiny agents of destruction are allowed to continue unabated, the whole edifice inches closer to collapsing. Denial only masks it.

The Grim Reality of our Situation is this:

We are a gridlocked nation befuddled by our method of decision making. Worse yet, we have "leaders" who have not yet attempted to tackle, let alone identify, the truly big issues that are dragging us down. It's not because these issues are hidden or are difficult to find. Indeed, they are so staggering in size and dimension that President after President has fallen into believing their own rhetoric that they are indeed powerless against them when in fact they are the ones who created them in the first place and can at any time withdraw their support.

These issues include, but are not limited to:

- *political parties that are more problematic than productive*

- *the influence of money in all aspects of our government*

- *an Electoral College that diminishes our voice in elections*

- *the giving away of most of our industrial base to China*

- *the pathetic positioning of the US as China's colony*

- *the emergence of fear–based policies in dealing with China*

- *the use of failed sanctions that only slow the advance of evil*

- *global politics that have us protect every border except ours*

- *the defeatist reasoning behind legitimizing illegal residents*

- *an economic system where the idle fare better than workers*

- *a health care system dominated by lawyers and insurers*

- *entrenched politicians who profit by making us powerless*

Wouldn't Ya Think?

Given that millions of us lost our homes and life savings, wouldn't ya think the crooks behind it would receive stiff sentences instead of bailout bonuses?

Given that our exports don't stand a chance against decades of China's unfair trade practices, wouldn't ya think we'd have import duties to level the playing field?

Given that it's been over 40 years since the OPEC oil embargo and energy crisis, wouldn't ya think we'd have a comprehensive energy plan in place by now?

Given that money has shifted power from the voters to big corporations, wouldn't ya think Congress would cleanse the temple and drive out the money changers?

Given that our oppositional two party system has now reached checkmate, game over, wouldn't ya think we'd have an intense dialogue on fine tuning democracy?

Given that this nation is as divided as were the old Civil War North and South, wouldn't ya think Congress would focus on healing our wounds as a nation?

Yet, none of it is happening. Why?

Politics as Sport

Instead of having a frank and open discussion on a topic before sitting down to take a vote, our politicians have hoodwinked us into believing we need to first toss it around and try to clobber each other in what can best be described as the great American game of political football.

Here's how it works. There are two teams complete with players, fans, cheerleaders and television commentators. The commentators whip the public into a feverish frenzy long before the contest begins, then serve as armchair quarterbacks throughout the process and remain on hand long after the contest is over.

On the field, each side focuses on scoring points against the other. This starts in the huddle where members devise plans to thwart the blocking and tackling tactics of their opponents. They can either pass it over their heads or make a run for it, barreling straight through their lines. Regardless of what they do, the opposing team has only one objective, to stop them cold. After so many downs, the other side takes possession of the ball and moves it back in the direction from whence it came.

Using the above as the framework for legislative achievement has some obvious drawbacks. First, and foremost, it divides everyone right down the middle and pits one half against the other. Second, the players run the risk of getting so caught up in the game that the issue itself is never given their full attention. And third, when both teams are evenly matched, as they are today, little progress can be achieved by either side.

Then, the whole thing bogs down into a stalemate. If the objective is sport, if the objective is drama, if the objective is increased television ratings and an ever-increasing flow of money from the fan base, then it is worth it. If, on the other hand, the objective is simply to move forward, then it is the worst possible way to succeed. Consider all of the injuries, the expenditure of time and the calories that are used to go a short distance only to have many things reversed when the other side gains control. There's got to be a better way to succeed as a democracy.

Political Parties
More of a Burden Than A Blessing

We all lose when we live in a divided country where the goal is not harmony and consensus, but rather victory over our opponents. It's like the saying, "We have met the enemy and he is us." To begin with, it means that only about half of us will ever be satisfied at any given time. It also guarantees that progress will always be slow and cumbersome if made at all. Take Amtrak as an example. Since its inception, it has been the darling of Democrats and the target of Republicans. Its funding depends on who is in office. When the Republicans are in control, funding is impeded and the whole thing deteriorates. Just when it is about to crumble, the Democrats return to power and the system is revitalized. Huge amounts of money are pumped back in, not only to restore what has fallen into disrepair, but also to sustain it through another dry spell. This is no way to run a railroad, let alone a country. Just ask defense contractors whose fortunes rise and fall on who occupies the Oval Office. It's terribly expensive to start up, shutdown and then start up again the same programs. It's like building a house and pausing just long enough for the plywood to rot a little before putting on the tar paper and shingles. Will it work? Yes. Will it pass inspection? Probably. Is it cost efficient with the best results? Definitely not.

We've been incorrectly led to believe that an adversarial relationship between two opposing parties is the only context in which a democracy can work. This simply isn't the case. Now, in a courtroom where there are only two possible outcomes, innocence or guilt, the sides are, by definition, opposed to one another. But we're not in a court of law. In fact, we're not even in the judicial branch of government. We're in the legislative branch, which, for good reason, is located on the other side of the street from the judicial. Here, consensus - not infighting - should be the goal.

We Don't Have To
Play This Game

Presently we're saddled with a government where getting even the simplest of things done requires making deals. Nothing is straightforward.

Everything has strings and questionable provisions attached, but no one wants to highlight or call attention to them. Legislators just hold their breaths and vote, ignoring the repugnant, in exchange for what they see as the overall good.

While it is true that we do not have the level of graft and corruption that hogtie many other nations, we do pay a high price for the way in which our government functions within our laws. Case in point is the late Sen. Robert Byrd, a Democrat from West Virginia. He used to brag about all of the money he got for his state merely by sitting on powerful Senate committees. Nothing got past him without his blessing and his blessing often came with a price. Now multiply this "pay to play" mentality by the number of elected officials we have in local, state and federal governments and it becomes readily apparent why our nation is dripping in red ink.

Congress and Automobile Repair

The best way to illustrate this absurdity is to liken it to car ownership. For the sake of argument, let's say that the members of Congress collectively own and share the responsibility for maintaining a car.

One member notices the brakes are getting a little soft. There is plenty of brake fluid in the reservoir, but the front pads are badly worn and in urgent need of replacement. When this person mentions it and asks for the funds to fix the problem, a fellow Congressman tells him that he has his vote, but if and only if new seat covers and an exhaust system are included as they are produced in his home state. Another, for similar reasons, promises to support funding the project, but again, if and only if the battery is replaced. (There is no need for that expenditure now, but given its age, who knows, the battery may in fact fail at any time.) Still another one pledges support, but asks that the radio be updated with a new voice activated CD player and surround sound speakers.

The Representative who sounded the alarm about the urgent safety issue of driving a vehicle with failing brakes begrudgingly goes along with all of these requests, as it is the only way to get the appropriation passed. The result is an old car with repairs totaling almost as much as the car did when it was new. The other options weren't necessary, but compared to the risk of driving a car with no brakes, it was truly a good deal.

All of these distasteful little things here and distasteful little things there add up and nickel and dime us to death. Worse yet, we're not only talking about pork barrel spending. This trading of political favors back and forth is a key element of the party system and permeates the entire legislative process. We'd be shocked if we knew not how many, but rather, how few items are voted on merely on the merits of that one item. I'm not sure which is more disturbing, that this flaw has gone unabated for so long or that no one has had the wisdom, or worse yet, the courage to tackle it.

We Are Denied a Full Range of Ideas

Another problem with "politics as usual" is that we don't get the depth of wisdom our tax dollars are funding. Supposedly, some of our best thinkers are sent to Washington for the sole purpose of working through the tough problems facing our nation. Yet, instead of hearing the host of creative solutions such a gathering should produce, we only hear the same tired, limited responses day after day, week after week, no matter whose mouth is actually moving.

On the one hand, we have the conservative perspective screaming at us in unison and on the other, we have the liberal perspective screaming at us in unison. These choruses are so repetitive and predictable that if we push the mute button on our remote controls, we know, without any volume, what they are saying simply by looking at the party affiliation posted on the screen.

This shouldn't be the case. We're not getting the breadth of perspectives we need to make astute decisions as a democracy. Instead, we are spoon fed the same endless drone of carefully crafted talking points. These rob the representatives of their individual voices and deny the nation urgently needed options. Sound bites based on scripted party lines aren't going to get us where we need to go.

Where would this country be if the founding fathers coalesced around only two viewpoints as soon as they arrived in Philadelphia? The American system of government never would have gotten off the ground. Thankfully, this didn't happen. Instead, incredibly imaginative ideas spurred more incredibly imaginative ideas. Sure, there were disagreements, but they were sincere disagreements that were given sincere consideration. The issues weren't about who came up with what proposal or who got the credit. They were bigger men than that as evidenced by the fact that they just kept at it. They hung in there together despite the blistering summer heat, with no air conditioning, wearing layers of formal wool and cotton clothing topped off with hot, scratchy wigs until finally, mercifully, the whole thing came together and a nation came to birth. Now, 200 plus years later, it is sadly newsworthy that a few of our leaders were able to bring themselves to sit next to each other at, of all things, the State of the Union Address.

One of the great ironies of democracy is that sometimes small constituencies end up wielding large amounts of power. This occurs when voting blocks are split down the middle with neither side having quite enough to carry the day.

In response, both sides then seek the support of smaller, less prominent groups and promise to adopt their issues in exchange for getting additional voters to the polls. This can lead to situations where "the tail wags the dog" and can be seen even now in regions of the country where Republicans and Democrats play to Hispanics voters in order to win elections.

Some would argue this is fair play in the ruthless game of politics. I'd argue that foreign policy and determining the citizenship of millions of people is no game. Anytime the smallest group is able to exercise leverage over the majority, the nation's interests are prone to suffer. If we had issue-based governance instead of party-based governance, this would never happen. There would be no motivation for forging alliances within the government if each representative left the party system and chose to only represent the people who sent him or her to Washington to objectively examine each issue solely on its merits and nothing else. Just think how dramatically improved the process would be if this were in fact the case.

There would be no more legislating according to the wishes of some caucus meeting behind closed doors, conspiring to pass or kill a bill. Some would say this is idealistic. Bad legislation will always get through as long as mere mortals cast the votes. While this is true, take away the sport of competing political parties and we'll see just how ineffective and wildly expensive they have been. In fact, some fear that if things are not corrected, and soon, they might in short order cost us our country.

Remember, just because a lot of things "have always been this way" doesn't make them right and certainly provides no legitimacy for them to continue. There is nothing in the Constitution saying we have to use political parties. The decision is entirely up to us. The good news, the truly wonderful news, is that making a change in our operating system doesn't require a revolution, massive protests in the streets, nor even a Constitutional Amendment. It doesn't even require somehow coming up with a majority of "Independent" legislators in either the House or Senate. All that is necessary is for us as to elect individuals wherever we can, whenever we can, who see the limitations of party politics and refuse to buy into them. In time, their presence will be like the leaven in the loaf, causing the whole thing to slowly rise to new heights.

Moving Toward Better Government

Time is of the essence. We should move with all due haste to clean house wherever possible. We need to replace as many politicians who have been involved in the game as possible and replace them with a fresh crop of individuals.

We do not need people of the same ilk, but rather people who think and act, not according to party lines, not according to power trips in Washington, not according to what will win re-election, but only according to what is good for the nation.

We need leaders with reasonable minds, good hearts and sound moral compasses that are able speak the truth in love while following their conscience and the directives of the people. That's all, and in time, other representatives will follow their examples or fade to silence until gradually, then all at once, we'll see a government of the people, by the people and for the people get traction.

There's no doubt about it. Parties are fun. They've even been a great source of amusement, particularly on the evening news, but they've cost us dearly and now threaten to reduce the greatest nation in human history to a second tier people. We won't survive this new, sobering, global configuration if we, like drunks at two out of control parties, weave back and forth from the left to the right and back again while other nations, more sober to the task, wait quietly in the wings for an opportunity to pounce.

Our most optimistic vision of our future can be found in our past. Benjamin Franklin was the consummate American. His life is still, to this day, a good example for the rest of us to follow. Listed below are but a few reasons for taking note of this friend of democracy.

1) **Ben Franklin was inventive and generous.** Many of his inventions were freely given to the public.

2) **He risked all he had to make things better.** This challenge to sacrifice is left to us today.

3) **When possible, Franklin sought the best for all,** as he felt to do less was to only partially succeed.

The Lost Art of Accommodation

Most people don't know this, but it was Benjamin Franklin who broke a stalemate that may have stopped the democratic experiment before it even got started. As history records it, the larger states understandably felt they should have the most representatives as they had the most territory and biggest populations. The smaller states, on the other hand, feared being squashed and drown out by the larger states. They had already experienced taxation without proper representation at the hands of the Crown and feared a repeat performance by the bigger states. Neither side would budge.

It was Benjamin Franklin who worked to see the validity of both sides of the same argument and came up with a solution. Instead of having only one legislative body, have two. The Senate would be comprised of an equal number of representatives from each state while the House of Representatives would have representation based on the state's population. Legislation would have to pass in both chambers before going to the President's desk for a signature. Forget about Franklin making a connection between lightning and electricity. It was his making a connection between opposing sides that was by far his greatest contribution to the American cause. He moved past the understanding of "winners" at the expense of "losers" to help form a more perfect union.

I was attending seminary in Berkeley, California when the Golden Gate Bridge celebrated its 50th anniversary. Officials closed the span and then opened it to pedestrian traffic at both ends at the same time. One end of the bridge opened with a high school marching band leading the way. At first, it all seemed well and good. Even the weather cooperated. The only problem was that no one had thought this thing through.

If they had, they would have realized that the overwhelming majority of walkers had made plans to be picked up once they reached the other side (as the span was too long for a round trip). Once these were established, there was no way to change course as there were no pay phones on the bridge and this was before most people had beepers, let alone cell phones. These folks weren't about to have friends or family members drive clear around the bay to pick them up at a pre-designated point on the other side only to find they weren't there. No, their path had been set, their destination chosen and there was no room for negotiation. They simply had to arrive.

Everything went smoothly until both groups met smack dab in the middle. Once there, what had started out as a leisurely stroll with balloons and dog leashes tied to the handlebars of baby strollers ended up becoming the pedestrian traffic jam from hell.

The poor high school marching band that had started off so gallantly ended up getting completely squashed in the ensuing gridlock. No one could budge an inch. The pressure just kept mounting and mounting as more and more piled in from both sides, pushing their way forward. It got so bad that people were actually throwing their bicycles into the pounding surf below. The total weight of the now stationary crowd flattened out the normal curvature of the bridge and more than a few wondered if the whole thing would collapse.

I relate this story because I think it is analogous to where this nation is today. We are a polarized society with a near 50/50 split when it comes to the electorate. We inevitably end up in the middle, but only to square off face to face against an equally intransigent group headed the opposite way. It is far from a joyous gathering. Rather, it is akin to getting stuck at loggerheads, dangling at a precarious height with a real fear of the whole structure falling out from under us.

What should have happened that fateful day, and should be happening every day in the halls of Congress, was to invite people to start in the middle and then move freely in either direction. Just as it is precisely the Golden Gate Bridge's ability to go with the flow instead of remaining inflexible that has made spanning the bay feasible all these years, so, too, it is in the allowance of traffic to flow in opposing directions that has made legislating the gulf that separates us an ongoing testimony to our union. The question shouldn't be "What's the best deal we can get for us?" any more than the personnel committee that was hiring my church secretary (Volume I) should have been asking "What's the least we can get away with offering?" No, in both cases, the question should have been, "What's the farthest we can go in meeting the needs and wishes of the other?"

A Few Small Changes toward Better Government

(1) Institute line item voting.

Under our current setup, bills are so large and cumbersome that no one has time to read them. This is an easy fix. Forget about getting a line item veto. Go to the root of the problem and get line item voting. That way each element is separate unto itself and there is no longer any excuse for supporting bad legislation.

(2) Don't require legislators to vote in person.

Have the bills disseminated early, via computers or on paper, so that elected officials can check off "yea" or "nay" on each provision. At the bottom they can sign off and hand them to a staffer who can then submit it on their behalf or be present on the chamber floor should the chair call for a voice vote. These simplified individual blocks of votes then become a part of their voting record that voters can scroll through when deciding whether or not to re-elect someone.

(3) Eliminate insider trading.

We don't want elected officials voting contrary to their better judgement. Doing so to pay off political favors is, in my mind, a clear conflict of interest and should be illegal. The only criteria that should be used in passing legislation is whether or not, standing on its own merits, that individual measure is for the good of the nation. Trading votes on Capitol Hill should be just as illegal as purchasing votes.

(4) Have Congress promote the nation's interests while state senators promote the state's interests.

Under the present system, each Congressional Representative's job description is in itself a conflict of interest. On the one hand, they are called upon to vote for what's best for the nation, while on the other, they are called upon to obtain what's best for their particular state. This is impossible as "no man can serve two masters."

The backroom politicking that results from this denies the legitimacy of any vote as the motivations are no longer pure. The solution is amazingly simple: discharge Congressional leaders from the task of securing the best position for their home state.

Instead, have state officials make their way to Capitol Hill to plead their cases before Congress when they have special requests like getting funding for a military base. When voting pertaining to that particular issue is taken, the Congressional representatives of that state should abstain from casting a ballot. In this way, all voting at the federal level is solely for what's in the very best interest of the entire nation, not a hodgepodge of tit for tat special favors and paybacks.

(5) No more "money-ocracy" …our present system of government where money rules.

Take all, and I mean all, of the money out of the democratic process and return the voice to the people. This means only a set number of dollars can be used in any campaign, period. Every dime of it will come from only one source, government coffers. No more political action committees, no more corporate funding of political ads. No more leaving for long periods to raise money to get re-elected. Corporations and special interests groups can address Congress, but not with checkbook in hand through lobbyists. Rather, they can speak when they are called upon to provide information, answer questions or participate in debates for all to hear. The only time they are given voice behind closed doors is when national security demands it. This will level the playing field and keep those with deep pockets from having an unfair advantage. If these simple measures are instituted, the voice of the electorate will regain strength and our political power will no longer be sold.

(6) We should choose our elected officials instead of having them choose us.

As it is now, parties have us declare whether we are Democrats or Republicans when we register to vote. This information is then transcribed onto a detailed map that shows politicians where their bastions of support lie and helps them decide how to draw the boundaries of Congressional Districts. As might be expected, the lines are shamelessly altered to give those already in power the best chance for re-election. This "redistricting" or "gerrymandering" the territories shouldn't be legal as it comes close to openly rigging an election. The obvious and ethical solution is to dump the redistricting process altogether and replace it with a fixed grid that accommodates shifts in population.

(7) Limit the run-up to elections

There should be a cap on the length of political campaigns. Currently, people are barely sworn in before opponents are announcing a bid for their seats. How can anything get done if we never move out of campaign mode long enough to focus on business? A year is more than enough time to communicate political platforms and positions especially in this age when they can be instantly disseminated through news and internet outlets. These campaigns should only be funded by the government, period. Once we agree to this course correction, power will be taken away from multinational corporations and given back where it belongs, to the people. From that time forward, our elected officials will no longer be required to dedicate so much of their time, talent and indeed, their very souls, just to get elected.

(8) Eliminate Term Limits!

Once in a while, a truly great leader emerges. The country shouldn't be denied the gifts that person has to offer simply because of an artificial method of ensuring a rotation of power. I mean, what's the ethical difference between allowing people to compete, on the basis of abilities alone, for a second or twenty-second term? In both scenarios, their voting record during over the past election cycle should be easy to access and the citizenry should decide.

With term limits, a sitting President runs the risk of being seen as a "lame duck" even before the confetti has fully landed from the second inaugural parade.

Or, just as bad, coming from completely the opposite end of the same continuum, the President may dig in his or her heels and become a bit authoritarian now that there are no more elections to win. So once again we have created yet another dualism with the President potentially feeling either all powerful or utterly powerless. Either way, this is a needlessly self-created quagmire that has the real potential of either increasing or decreasing the authority of the office.

Furthermore, if there are term limits, adversaries here at home and abroad may be tempted to just "wait out the clock" and not respond to the President's initiatives as they know that one way or the other, someone new will soon occupy the Oval Office.

(9) Hold a special election should tragedy strike.

While it is wise to have an immediate assumption of leadership should a President die in office, I believe a special election for a permanent successor should be held.

(10) Eliminate conflicts of interest in elections.

Without question, there was a clear conflict of interest in having then Governor of Florida, Jeb

Bush, even remotely involved in the 2000 Presidential Elections. Even if there were no improprieties, the mere risk of appearing to use his office to his brother's advantage dictated that he should have been required to do what every judge does when there is even a hint of a conflict of interest, namely remove him or herself from having anything to do with the matter.

(11) Eliminate foreign money to all campaigns and all gifts to present, past or future officials.

The same China that gave, and later returned under scrutiny, money to Bill Clinton's campaign, gained control of the Panama Canal during his term in office. As President, Bill Clinton never even raised an eyebrow. Coincidence? Or money well spent?

(12) Make All Votes Equal by Taking Two Steps:

Cast Votes on Same Day/ Dump Electoral College

These two steps alone will go a long way in restoring our democracy. Under the present system, voters in Florida have far more say in electing a President than in other places. This is true for two reasons. The first reason is that the state has set up an early primary. The results from Florida's primary often determine who will stay in the race and who will drop out long before citizens in other locations get to cast an encouraging or discouraging vote.

Secondly, because of its size and number of electoral delegates, voters in Florida yield far more power than people in states like North Dakota or Delaware that have fewer votes in the Electoral College.

The fix is simple. Have two election days, one for the primary election and one for the general election. Have each vote cast on those days carry equal weight so that it doesn't matter where the vote is cast just as long as it is cast by a registered American voter.

(13) No More Filibusters

The premise of a democracy is that all voices have equal weight. Filibusters fly in the face of this as they give a single legislator the right to bring the process to a screeching halt while he or she barters for even more power. Wheeling and dealing is the problem, not the solution.

(14) *No More Lobbyist Loot!*

Question: Who gets paid the most attention? Answer: The people who pay the most to get it.

Our whole system of government has opened itself wide to the influence of money. As a result, we the citizens, not the multinational corporations who employ armies of lobbyists, not the foreign governments who donate to campaigns, but rather the rest of us, as in "We the People," are the ones who pay the high price for this allowance.

And when I say that we are "paying the price," I'm talking about actual dollars and cents. For the only reason, I repeat, the *only* reason, donors give to candidates and their election committees is to make their influence felt. To put it bluntly, they want the same thing any child wants, namely to get their own way.

After these "donors" are done hosting the golfing junkets and throwing the parties, "We the People" end up paying to clean up the mess. That price is always high, because there is nothing dirtier to clean up after than a government that allows the influence of money to get into its method of doing business. It taints the whole legislative process. Unfortunately, our government is just dripping with money.

How much money has found its way to our nation's Capital? It's hard to say exactly, but ask any elementary school child and they can tell you that originally Washington, D.C. was built on a swamp. (Go figure). Now, I don't know of any swamps with hills in them, do you? There aren't any. Come to think of it, there aren't any valleys in swamps, either. Legend has it that this was precisely the reason they chose to locate the seat of our government there in the first place. Our founding fathers thought that building the capital city on a swamp would mean that it would always be on the level. (So much for the best of intentions.)

Over time, however, something happened that even the founding fathers didn't anticipate, namely the infusion of money. It just started pouring in. Politicians tried to line their pockets with it, but that didn't work as they usually got caught. So they did the only thing they knew to do. They just sat on it, and in time, that pile of money grew into an entire hill of money that we've now come to know and affectionately refer to as Capitol Hill. How much money has piled up there? It's hard to reckon, but we increasingly hear it said that "Washington is just full of it."

Perhaps, this explains how they could build such a great big, heavy Capitol Building complete with that massive dome (extra storage) and yet not have it sink into the swamp. Apparently, money is holding the whole thing up. In fact, money is its only foundation. Foundation? Just listen to me, going along with their little story! I should certainly know better than to take their words at face value. But then maybe there is something behind it. After all, more and more of us are seeing the same thing. More and more of us are "holding these truths to be self-evident" that there is no real foundation on Capitol Hill other than the Almighty Dollar. Why else would commentators be forever telling us that not just the building, but the entire Hill is leaning first to the right and then to the left and back again? I don't know of anything that can cause something to sway that much unless the reports are right, that our government has raised itself to new heights, but under the fine granite, it is akin to a swamp covered cesspool filled in with filthy loot.

Now, I'm no structural engineer, but given the shiftiness of money and the speed with which it moves, I think it is the absolute worst thing to use as a foundation. It's even shiftier than building a house on the proverbial sand that Jesus talked about. For money is so, what's the word? Fluid. Money is so fluid that we even talk about floating a loan, or letting the currency float until it finds its equilibrium. And we want to build on it? It all seems terribly risky given the fact that it's so slick that it can be sent around the world, via Western Union, as quick as lightning. And not only can it skedaddle, it can completely disappear. How many people do you know that scrimped and saved all their lives so that they could put just enough aside of it to build a little nest egg. Then one night, they went to bed feeling all safe and secure like a bug in a rug, only to wake up the next morning and find that poof, it was gone. And do I mean gone! Apparently the market crashed and everything was gone without so much as a trace.

No one has the billions that were lost in the crash of '29. They weren't stolen and put into someone else's account. That would have been more understandable and easier to fix. No, those billions simply vanished. They disappeared quicker than kids called upon to wash the dishes. Soon afterward, we had a housing crisis and good, hardworking people found themselves on the street. When I ponder all of this,

I'm all the more certain that I don't want my life to be built on money and I don't want the government that is there to protect and preserve my life, liberty and pursuit of happiness built on it either. We are now paying the price, the tragic price of such an error.

It's absolutely imperative that we immediately get every penny, nickel, dime and dollar out of not only every campaign, but every political activity under the sun. Until we do so, we're back to square one and the intolerable reality of taxation without representation which every reasonable patriot knows is wrong.

The preservation of democracy and the assurance of citizen participation should be job one of any President. Time on the golf links or hanging out with the elite or financially well-heeled so as to get financial contributions to win elections is certainly no excuse for ensuring the integrity of a government of the people, for the people and by the people.

Many Citizens Truly Believe We've Gone Back to Taxation Without Representation

How Bad has it Gotten?

Drones are clearly a major security threat and fracking is, in my opinion, nothing short of a looming environmental nightmare. Yet, to the date of the printing of this book, I'm not aware of the government promoting much public discourse on either topic. I find this to be both tragic and frightening in a supposedly democratic nation. In both cases, I think it points to the reality that money is stealing power away from the people.

Additionally, Many of Us Wonder:

Why are billions and billions given, year after year, to hostile nations that take the money and then turn around and thumb their nose at us? I find the practice repugnant. It simply has got to stop. If a country wants our help, there are things we want in return like a commitment to democratic reform. If these demands are not met, then the check will no longer be in the mail.

No More
Leaving Goodies at the Door

How much foreign aid is diverted to enrich the crooks at the top and never gets to those who are in desperate need of it? The answer is, too much. No more. We will deliver aid in such a way that it gets to its rightful destination and that it is abundantly clear that the gift is coming from us.

A Winning Strategy
for Combating Terrorism

Oct. 31, 2014, shots rang out on Parliament Hill in Ottawa, leaving Nathan Cirillo dead. He was a ceremonial sentry at Canada's National War Memorial. Following the attack and subsequent death of the shooter, the mother of Michael Zehaf-Bibeau, a self-described Muslim Jihadist, publicly denounced the incident and apologized for her son's actions.

Once again the terrorists had landed a solid punch, escaped to the supposed arms of virgins on the other side and left us with no opportunity for redress. All that was left for us to do was to begrudgingly accept his mother's apologies, comfort those impacted by the attack and brace for the loss of yet more civil liberties in a vain attempt to protect ourselves.

This scenario is certainly not new. Since September 11, 2001, this has been our ongoing response to terrorist acts.

I, For One, Do Not Accept the Major Premise of This Failed Policy

People are not hatched. They are not left to fend for themselves as best they can like lone turtles in the sand. No, they are born into families, into communities. Furthermore, individuals may be motivated by misguided self-interests to commit crimes, but they go to war for one reason and one reason alone and that reason is to better the lot of the communities into which they are born.

I submit that this gunman's acts were not, as they would have us believe, the act of a single, depraved individual. Rather, they were the composite sum total result of all the hate filled messages given him from his earliest years right up to the moment he pulled the trigger. This is based upon the simple fact that thousands of Muslims, even now, with the benefit of full disclosure of his actions, hold him up as a hero and would gladly repeat the same offense were they given the opportunity.

I cannot help but believe that though apologetic while in the media spotlight, chances are the mothers of many of these militants are privately proud of their sons and that these men are revered in their home towns in much the same way we look upon those who have lost children fighting for causes we hold dear. This undercurrent of albeit tacit approval is fully comprehended by the next generation of young boys who in turn are anxious to take up arms that they might become the next generation of heroes.

We Have Unwittingly Set Up
an Unwinnable Situation

Until we accept the above premises, that terrorists are not merely individuals acting as "lone wolves" but rather are offshoots or extensions of the communities that created them, they will continue to operate with the reckless abandon of soldiers who go to war confident that retaliation for their actions will never hit home.

Indeed, they behave like children who throw a punch, knowing that all they have to do is run and hide behind their mother's apron strings. Those apron strings constitute the very same criminal justice system that was originally designed to protect innocent people from those who would intentionally and willfully harm them, not the other way around.

Here's how they use it to their advantage. After ruthlessly attacking, without the slightest provocation, unarmed and hapless civilians in a manner that exceeds any previously held estimation of savage barbarism, terrorists turn around and demand the full range of rights and privileges of a legal system that will dole out millions of taxpayer dollars to ensure they are granted a fair trial. Chances are the verdicts that are eventually reached will in all likelihood never be carried out as the same legal system views even the most painless of executions by lethal injection as cruel and unusual punishment.

Conversely, if the terrorists do happen to die during their initial assault, the whole matter is immediately dropped as we then maintain there is no one else to hold accountable. Either way, if they live or if they die, they seem to have escaped the level of wrath they unleashed on us. Thus, it is a one-sided conflict.

Moving Toward a Solution

Terrorists know full well that they are doing much more than merely committing crimes. Indeed, even the intellectually challenged can recognize the difference between a crime and an act of war. Crimes are offenses committed against individuals or groups of individuals while wars are larger in scope, hellish in nature and waged against entire societies and nations. As if we really need further proof of the difference, we need only look at how the perpetrators view their own activities. When we do this, we soon realize that even they speak in terms of jihad or a "holy war."

If a People Declares War on Us, We'd Be Foolish Not to Accept Their Assessment

Israel understands this. For decades it has been Target One, yet, even with its immediate proximity to those who seek to do it harm, it exists in relative safety. Why is that? I believe it is because they accept the scope of the conflict. They affirm that every bomb blast is an act of war committed by a warrior. In this realization, they do not call upon the police, but rather the military to deal with it. The military's response is to try to figure out who is behind the bombing, then drive a tank over and knock down their house. This suddenly changes the equation from that of a child being able to throw a punch and escape retaliation by running to the protective arms of the legal system to having the perpetrators themselves suffer real consequences. Families that once harbored terrorists now keep a close eye on their children lest their actions literally bring the house down.

They Truly Have Instigated a "War of Terror"

Since terrorists knew they didn't have sufficient wealth, soldiers or weapons to ever become an imposing military presence, they didn't even bother making the attempt. Instead they sidestepped the whole process altogether, "cut to the chase" and focused their attention on trying to create the same level of fear that the Russians felt when Napoleon's forces were advancing on St. Petersburg or Europe experienced when Hitler initiated his blitzkrieg or lightning war.

Terrorists aren't crazy. They're ingenious. Their objective is and has always been the same as every other power player, to get enough clout to become a force to be reckoned with. How they get there is ultimately irrelevant if the outcome is the same, namely to generate enough fear in others to get people to sit up, take notice and one day give in to the demands they place upon them. That is why terrorists are out to produce a level of fear so deep, so dreadful, that it can only be described as terror.

Unpredictability is Their Greatest Weapon

I firmly believe the fundamental, core component of this terror is the unpredictable nature of it all. There are no rules of engagement or codes of conduct. It has no designated battle lines, no uniformed soldiers. It can be initiated by anyone, anywhere, anytime in any number of unpredictable ways. There is no truly safe place for people to hide and take refuge. It is precisely this element of surprise, this potential for the utter banishment of serenity from our lives that makes terrorism such a scary opponent.

Yet, we need not be afraid. This challenge is definitely winnable, if we have leadership that is wise enough to figure it out and courageous enough to fight it.

Looking to the Past and Present to Chart a Future

(A Brief Aside) Congress should, and I'm serious about this, either appropriate the funds to buy out the History Channel or create one of its own. I say this because the cornerstone of any healthy democracy is an intelligent, well informed citizenry.

The knowledge base this network has acquired over the years is nothing short of phenomenal. The problem is the History Channel, for commercial reasons, shelved just about all of it and has since replaced it with endless hours upon endless hours of programing about pawn stores and the virtue of roaming the country looking for antiques and collectibles.

Had it not abandoned its original mission, perhaps we'd know some things today about Islam that might be helpful. For example, most people wrongly confuse the Spanish Inquisition with the Crusades. Though both were horrific, bloody affairs, the first was in fact an attempt to get people to subscribe to a certain theological view. The second, on the other hand, was more about access. Back then, people, including Christians, made religious pilgrimages. As Islam spread, access to the Holy Lands became threatened and the Crusades were launched to prevent this control of the region from spreading even further.

Part of the reason we blend the two is because Billy Graham used the word "crusade" to describe his efforts at spreading the Gospel. Put all of this into the same blender and factor in our knee jerk assumption that the West, particularly America, is always on the wrong side of everything and we end up with some ideas that are a bit off base. Thus the need for the kind of programming the History Channel once provided. (Now, Back to the Topic at Hand)

The Day a Flea
Took Control of a Horse

A group of thug militants appeared on the world stage 36 years ago when they stormed the US Embassy in Iran and took hostages with nothing more than a bunch of machine guns.

In terms of size and firepower against the United States, they were a bit like the flea that gained control of the horse. How did they do it? Simple. They knew that while we might be the biggest kid on the block, we were also the most ethical, the most principled and, yes, the most Sunday Schooled and it's precisely this that was their ticket to pinning us to the ground.

How did it happen? Correct me if I'm wrong, but just as some time ago we convinced ourselves we were too sophisticated for tawdry factory work, that we could make money without ever producing anything and therefore gave away all of our factories, so, too, we've not only convinced ourselves, but also put out the message to all the world that the USA is too big, too advanced, too mature and too civilized to stoop to something as barbaric, as primitive as war.

Yes. It may be true that we have the most advanced missile systems on the planet, "but with them comes the awful ethical responsibility of setting an example for the world"… and therefore will never, ever use them. Once that word was put forth, our advanced weaponry became about as useless as a high tech parking lot for advanced rocketry.

The whole dynamic reminds me of the 1940's and 50's when bodybuilders were fairly new on the scene. Back then, they were openly derided as "pretty boys" by the rough and tumble, street hardened scrappers from the likes of the lower East Side and the Bowery. They sized them up and knew these massive guys had enough strength and muscle to crush them with their bare hands, but would never do it as they were too preoccupied with their appearance to risk getting a tooth knocked out or suffering a disfigurement that would detract from posing in front of a mirror.

As it turned out, the street fighters were all about blood sport while the bodybuilders were all about image and posturing. That's just the way it was. So the littler guys with their Napoleon complexes derided and openly made fun of the much larger and more imposing body builders; and as outlandish as it seems, they consistently got away with it.

The strength of the brawlers, their secret weapon, was not their strength at all. Rather, it was the knowledge that the bigger guys would take a lot of abuse and never punch back. That's exactly what's going on with these terrorists.

Look at what each side has to bring to the fight. On the one side, we have a comparatively small contingent armed with only machine guns and crudely crafted roadside bombs. On the other side, the largest, most advanced military the world has ever known. Yet, who dominated the field? The Iranians held not only 52 diplomats, but our entire nation, captive for 444 days.

What Finally Ended the Iranian Hostage Crisis? The Answer: Good Old Fashioned Fear

As long as kind and principled Jimmy Carter was in the White House, the Iranians had nothing to fear. When Ronald Reagan came to town, the gig was up.

They knew he had no compunction about bombing the living daylights out of them if that's what it took and so out of fear of what might happen, they released the hostages the very morning he was sworn in.

Now, here we are, four decades and a number of wars later and the same terrorists that stormed the US Embassy in Iran have gone from outsiders to positions of leadership at the top. Neither they nor North Korea, another nuclear power want-to-be, have so much as a single nuclear device, yet, we're the ones who are trembling in our boots. Why?

The Reason We Are Losing the War on Terror

Quite simply, we are losing "The Terrorist War" because they're doing a better job at scaring us than we are at scaring them. Think about it. We've never threatened to wipe them from the face of the Earth, but they've never ceased talking about annihilating Israel. Is it wise to allow a nation to repeatedly make such dire threats and never throw some cautionary words back at them? I think not.

I'm just curious as to why we've never said back to them, "You'd better pray that you don't ever try something so foolish, because if you do, we will stand with Israel and you will be tossed aside and left on what Reagan once referred to as "the ash heap of history."

"Oh, that's terrible," some will say. "How could we even think of uttering saying such a thing?" And on and on it goes.

Here's my real question. Where's the leadership been? Up until now, these two bit bullies have thoroughly spooked us when they are the ones who should be worried.

Terrorists have not only threatened us, they've actually busted our lip open a few times and what has been our response? We're like the kid whose momma takes out her handkerchief, wipes away the blood, straightens out his cute little necktie, and as she combs his hair with her fingers and kisses him on the forehead tells him, "Now, don't you stoop down to their level. Carry yourself like a man so that I can be proud of you... and oh, by the way, start taking a different way to and from school."

Am I wrong? How so? We're the ones who have lost our civil liberties. Our phones are now tapped, our correspondence read, our movements tracked. We're practically strip searched every time we go to the airport. We can't even carry knapsacks or beverage coolers into crowded stadiums.... and we call ourselves Americans?

All this while the terrorists go unabated. They're actually growing in number and why wouldn't they be? We've never struck back. Oh, sure, the Bushes (in addition to plunging us into economic catastrophe every time they've been in the White House) have unilaterally thrown a few wars, but not one of them have had the slightest connection to fighting terrorism.

Any Middle East expert or child forced to repeat the fourth grade can tell you that before we entered Iraq, the country had absolutely no terrorist activity at all, period. Going into Iraq under the ridiculous guise of fighting terrorists after the 911 attacks made about as much sense as us today bombing Red Square to rid the world of Nazis. It is just about as illogical.

No, the problem is that we have responded to their war of utter unpredictability by being utterly predictable. Can you imagine being in a war where a person can lob a hand grenade and then not duck for cover, but rather immediately stand up and start walking around looking for a good defense attorney? What? They have no money to hire one? No problem. By the time it gets to court in a few years, the best of the best will be on their defense team with the American taxpayer picking up the tab.

Even if our government's side prevails in Court, the worse that can happen to them is the loss of the one person. That person can wipe out an entire city, or if Iran gets the bomb, an entire nation and the worse that will come of it is that he or she will suffer. Not at all a bad deal, is it? They can wipe out untold numbers of civilians, but we will never get more than one or perhaps a handful of convictions in a court of law.

Winning Hearts and Minds?

Why are social media companies allowing themselves to be used as the primary tool for recruiting people to join Isis? As much as I hate it when people always default to Adolf Hitler as a yardstick of ultimate evil, I am going to do just that and ask, what, if any, responsible media outlet would broadcast Hitler's propaganda today? The answer is simple. I can't think of any. Why? It is because even now it is able to incite hatred so intense as to rekindle anew unspeakable crimes against humanity.

If this is the case, how for the love of planet Earth can we even begin to justify the promulgation of such vitriolic hate mongering through social media? If the founders of these companies, the Zuckerbergs, Andersons, Dorseys, Pages and Brins of the world don't get it and continue to insist on their networks protecting terrorists' freedom of speech, then it is way past the time for governments the world over to put an end to it before further denying our personal freedoms through opening one more letter, tapping one more phone call, making one more of us practically undress at one more airport, put one more soldier in a uniform, fit one more wounded soldier with a prosthetic limb or play taps at one more funeral.

Listen to the news, read the paper. This is a war, it is they themselves who have declared it. We had better take notice and now act to try to deescalate it before it spreads past the quagmire of the Middle East to their next publicly declared target, the cities of Europe.

Who Wouldn't Go to War With Us?

Going to war with America is a pretty safe proposition. We are the last ones on the planet to acknowledge that we are under attack. As just mentioned, we deny it by trying the perpetrators as individuals in a court of law. Even worse, more often than not, we act as though nothing has happened. Just ask the Chinese who have been launching cyber-attacks on both military and civilian targets for years. Our only response, that I'm aware of, is that we've kept them on our most favored nations list. On the other side, if we accidentally miss a target, we are quick to pay big bucks to the families that have been wronged, but have some of the worst care for own veterans who are maimed for life. Need I go on?

When Will We Realize Even If We Stay on The Yellow Brick Road, It Will Only Take Us to A Fictitious Land Called Oz?

We might be arrogant and foolish enough to actually believe we can win a war by moral persuasion, but it doesn't change the fact that the very same people who strap bombs on children and send them into Crowded markets are the ones who now, as I write these words, are inching closer to obtaining legal protection for their nuclear ambitions. Having already lost our nerve, have we now also lost our minds? Why on earth would we sign onto such a deal? The argument is that by doing so, we have access to inspections, while a military response such as bombing Iran will only drive them underground. Are they kidding? Surely Neville Chamberlain could have done better.

The whole thing is eerily similar to the fallacious argument that by continuing to trade with China, not only do we have access to a formerly closed off country, but they have access to our democratic way of doing things and will easily be won over. Great! It's been almost half a century; where's this move to democratic reform? They are now curbing their citizens' access to the internet. Yet, our policy remains.

The people with whom we are dealing in Iran have not only verbalized, but demonstrated over and over again an utter disregard for human life. Quite simply, they are not to be trusted with nuclear materials of any kind for any reason, period.

So, Where Do We Go From Here?

1) We need to get off our moral high ground and realize the bottom line, namely that this is a war complete with bombs. Anytime bombs are used and nations are threatened, it isn't an individual committing a crime, it is an act of war and it shouldn't be adjudicated in a Court of Law.

2) Next, we need to realize that wars are not fought until the assailed are sick and tired of them. No, to the contrary, they are fought until the instigators get so thoroughly sick and tired of them that they will do just about anything to stop them.

3) Aggressors have no reason to stop hostilities when they are winning. Why would they stop? No, it is only after they see that it is to their ultimate disadvantage to continue that thy will call a halt to their participation.

4) We will never stop this madness until they are far more afraid of us until we are of them. The populations we are dealing with are not powerless. Look at the massive, massive,

massive turnout there was in street protests over their rage at cartoonists. They let their voices be heard. The fact that no such street protests of any kind took place in the aftermath of 911 or mass beheadings of innocent aid workers says to me they are far from innocent bystanders. None of it would happen without their support.

The cessation of their activities will only come when these same folks take to the streets and demand an end to the brutality. Whether we like it or not, that won't happen until they live under the same terror that they are dishing out to us and the rest of the world. They are the ones in the driver's seat. Once they cry enough, then and only then will the madness stop.

Lest You're Still Not Convinced, Let Me Try again...Yes, It Is that Important!

We won't negotiate with terrorists, but will negotiate with terrorist states. How does that work? I don't know. Something doesn't add up here. We take great pride in claiming the moral high ground for not negotiating with terrorists. That's all fine and good.

I, along with most Americans, most certainly don't have any problems with this and actually support it.

What I don't understand, however, is how we then go to feeling OK about negotiating with a terrorist state such as Iran. Am I missing something here? What am I not understanding? Iran, for decades, has made it abundantly clear that as a government, a county, it is committed to the "annihilation of Israel." That's their words, no one else's, and they have never been uttered by accident, as in a slip of the tongue. No, they have been stated over and over and over again in a clear, matter of fact fashion. Now, let's stop and really think about this for a moment, because it really is that important.

Annihilation. Next to eternal damnation, it is perhaps the scariest, most devastating concept human language can convey. It far exceeds even the dark loathsome pathology of the Nazis who had absolutely no compunction about exterminating Jews. As hard as it may be to imagine, this goes much, much farther in that it bespeaks the total eradication and removal of virtually everything, not just human life, so that when accomplished no people, no structures, no nature, nothing, but nothing remains.

The only, repeat only way to wipe everything so totally away is through the use of nuclear force and yet, here we are negotiating with the same state about "their right" to have a nuclear program. To even enter into such a discussion in the first place boggles the mind. That alone is bad enough, but then to be so easily hoodwinked as to accept any deal of any kind with the devil himself and then go on and suggest to potential victims that such an agreement is the only way to monitor the other side's activities so as to enable us to provide their protection is the height of repugnant folly. This isn't funny. This is serious business. Not just the citizens of Israel, not just the citizens of New York and London, Madrid and Moscow, but the citizens of any community of any density of population should be trembling in their boots, for this is far, far, far more dangerous than during the darkest hours of the Cuban Missile Crisis or any brush up during the Cold War. This a borderless war. It is about global domination. All of us, repeat, all of us the world over are at risk, for they don't need missile delivery systems, they don't even need a military. All they need is enough nuclear grade material to fill a brief case. That brief case can be left anywhere in the world by any zealot convinced there are virgins waiting for him in eternity and it's checkmate, game over. Tell me, what are you as a citizen going to do today to get our "leaders" to understand that folks like this shouldn't be handling anything even remotely connected to nuclear materials? Well? Don't just sit there. Pick up the phone, send an email, and choose wisely at the voting booth. Do all of the above, but for the love of God, for the sake of humanity, do something!

It's One Thing to Kick a Can Down the Road...

People do it all of the time. There is no real harm in it. All that happens is that the same issues are dealt with a little later on. It's quite another thing to start a snowball rolling down a hill, for it grows larger and larger and more formidable the further it travels. What started out as something innocuous can soon mushroom into something that is not only dangerous, but nearly impossible to stop.

Correct me if I'm wrong, but Iran is no empty aluminum can. Every year we don't take decisive action we allow it to become more dangerous and threatening. Like that snowball, it expands by pulling more and more into itself the further it travels. If we think the Iran of today is scary, just wait until we see the Iran of five or ten years from now.

As for Putting Putin in His Place

Administration after administration have stood silently by as this former KGB boss has slowly, but surely, worked to reverse what had been a steady movement toward true, across the board, democratic reform. We've known about his intimidation of political enemies, his gradual reduction of freedom of the press and his manipulation of the democratic process that has enabled him to remain the chief power broker despite the name changes on the door. Yet, in spite of all of this, our response has been pitifully absent. In real terms, it has been all but nonexistent.

Now, Putin, with Crimea under his belt, is threatening more invasions, and what has been our response? As of the writing of these words, it has been twofold. First, we have had our own government officials running to the microphones and quoting Putin's promise that he really and truly won't invade anywhere else. Boy that really makes me sleep better at night … and to think that Putin wants to squelch freedom of the press! Why would he want to do that when he is using it to have our leaders repeat his lies?

Our second approach is just as laughable. It is the implementation of sanctions. Are we serious? I cannot think of a situation where aggressors haven't used them to their advantage. They have rightfully come to regard them as a guaranteed time-out, not for them, but for us. Indeed, when we issue them all that registers in the ears of the offenders is our declaration that we will "give them time to work." This they accept as our promise not to strike while we are still evaluating the effectiveness of these measures.

When we use sanctions, we become like the hockey team that takes itself off the ice and sits in the penalty box while the other side carries on much as before (except perhaps a little more discreetly), firm in the assurance that nothing will be done to them militarily. What a windfall for them! They know that if they tone it down a bit and play cat and mouse, they can keep right on going without any fear of physical harm. This sense of security, of not fearing for their lives, rests not so much in their ability to protect themselves as in something even stronger, the belief that we won't break our word.

In The Final Analysis

Sanctions are to them little more than a cost of doing business, a fine, and an expensive, but foolproof way of guaranteeing their safety while they continue to operate under the protective umbrella we have offered them. Do they work? Sure they do, but only for the other side, as again, I can't think of a single instance where we have come out on top. Just look at North Korea and Iran. Thanks to sanctions, their economies are stagnant, but so what? Their leaders couldn't care less as they themselves continue to live like kings.

Both countries have made incredible strides in developing their nuclear capabilities and now we have far more reason to fear them than they have ever had to fear us. Ultimately, it all boils down to this: sanctions only slow evil's hideous advance. Perhaps that's why Webster's lengthy definition of "sanction" also includes the words "support, encouragement; approval," as in the sanctioning of a certain behavior.

What Then Will Stop
Invading Armies
in Their Tracks?

For seven decades we have borne the ginormous cost of stationing troops in Germany and the rest of Europe. Have we done it to protect us from the Nazis? I don't think so. Rather, it has been to guarantee the safety of Europe from Cold War Soviet advances. Since then, we have talked Ukraine into surrendering its nuclear arsenal by promising that we would protect them from any incursions. Well, here we are. They have been invaded by Russia and yet we have not provided them the protection we promised. How utterly pathetic is that?

To me, it is all the more grotesque given that we, at this very minute, are also pressuring Israel to trust us to defend them from Iran. Yet, year after year, we have watched Iran inch closer and closer to a nuclear bomb with sanctions only slowing, never stopping their progress. My point is this: until we back up our promises, our word is worthless.

To talk people into surrendering their defensive weapons with the promise that we will protect them and then not fulfill that promise is to sink to a new low. Such inaction is utterly amoral inasmuch as it makes us no different than those who lead the sheep to the slaughter.

The Hispanics

Even though I recognize and affirm that there are North Americans, Central Americans and Latin Americans, for the sake of brevity and readability, I have adopted the common practice of referring to citizens of the USA as "Americans." This, to my mind, is an acceptable abbreviation as only the United States includes the word "America" in its lengthy formal name.

Secondly, while angered by those who have sneaked across our borders, I welcome those who respect the rule of law and wish to join us by following due process.

Mature thinking tells us that
it is one thing to help a friend
and it is totally another
to lose one's identity
in the process.

The MAS H Generation

We live in odd times. It's as though what our teachers told us is coming true, that like ancient Rome, no foreign power can topple us. No, we can only fall from within.

Alan Alda's character did such a masterful job of training us who grew up in what I now think of as the "MASH Generation" to be cynically suspicious of all things American, that, for the first time in our history, we tend to automatically assume that we are always in the wrong and that if we aren't, then at the very least, we are doing good for all of the wrong reasons.

At the same time, we tend to naively assume the exact opposite of everyone else. We always, always, always give them the benefit of the doubt and are as blind to their shortcomings as we to the good things we routinely do. This is so deeply imbedded in our way of thinking that we now have the whole thing backwards with us assuming we are guilty until we can prove otherwise.

Are There Only "Ugly Americans" Or Can the Label be Universally Applied?

The questions remain: *Why do we find it so hard to be universally fair? Why are we so blooming' accommodating when it comes to others and at the same time so ruthlessly hard on ourselves? I* don't know, but hopefully we can at least realize that only a good and compassionate people indulge in such labored self-criticism when looking in a mirror only to then turn the other cheek when looking at others.

Though we may find it distasteful to speak less than favorably of others, the fact remains that many arrive in this nation expecting total accommodation on our part to make up for a total lack of effort on their part. Nowhere is this more evident than in the refusal of some, not all, but some to learn the prevailing language and become one of us. To me, that's as distasteful as seeking to be adopted into a family and refusing to accept the family name. It is, objectively speaking, as rude as it is wrong.

A Question of Language

In order to access a computer's software, all of us commit ourselves to learning the language of computers, no questions asked, no protest made. In order to play a musical instrument such as a piano or violin, we learn the language of musical notation, no questions asked, and no protest made. When we enter a court of law, we utilize the framework and terminology of the court. There are no questions asked, no protest made. The reason we do all of these things is simple, we accept and respect the language of that particular domain. If we want to enter into it, if we want to access it, then we acquiesce to the fact that we'd better learn that language.

Adopting an official state language and allowing it to operate on one mode of expression is an acknowledgment of the State's right to enjoy freedom of expression. If people want to access governmental services, they must take the steps, as we do in the examples mentioned above, to learn the language of its expression. Remember, the State is the issuer of law and law prides itself on exactitude and minutia of meaning. Indeed, lives and generations of lives turn on the interpretation of a single word or phrase in the law. This is certainly true when it comes to the Constitution. Here we are, still struggling with the legal constructs that the Constitution presented in one language, English, well over 200 years ago. It is folly to think that our system of governance can cope with and adopt the language of every new person who arrives.

Just think of the opening for legal challenges that would be created if the government tried. Leap ahead twenty years and imagine some slick lawyer figuring out that a ballot initiative voted on years prior needs to be overturned and reversed retroactively to when it became law because it was misrepresented in one of the numerous languages that are currently used on the California ballot. Higher Courts quickly agree, apply a strict "constructionist" interpretation to the ordinance and interpret the claim by the letter of the law. Wham, millions are paid out in damages, lower court cases are subsequently reviewed and overturned and on it goes from there. It soon escalates into every lawyer's dream and our worst nightmare. Let's not go down the road. Legalisms are difficult enough as they are currently presented, with the use of just one language. Let's not make it exponentially more difficult by revisiting the tower of Babel. Let's keep it simple. When it comes to language, let's embrace the charge President Kennedy put so well, "Ask not what your country can do for you. Ask what you can do for your country."

Hispanic immigrants challenge our fundamental definition of what it means to be an American by:

1) Self identifying around a "foreign" language.

2) Coalescing around and voting for issues that only favor Hispanics and not the whole country.

When a person becomes an American, they pledge their allegiance to this nation. We all understand this. What I don't understand is how Hispanic voters can put Hispanic concerns first, over and above the concerns they have for the United States. As if to add insult to injury, both parties go right along with this crowd and play up to them in a grotesque effort to do whatever they can for their votes just so they can get re-elected. Why come to a country that prides itself, above all else, on being a great melting pot if you have no intention of joining the mix? Unless, of course, it is with the hope that everyone will eventually accept your steadfast refusal to change and/or make changes to accommodate you.

Something is terribly wrong when the new arrivals in a land flat out refuse to change. Why? Why is that so wrong? It is because at some point accommodation has to take place in order for at least some level of communication to occur. If those coming in don't learn the prevailing language and their numbers swell, then look out. It is only a matter of time before help wanted ads insist on only having bilingual applicants, or worse yet, having only those who speak Spanish apply.

Ask the natives of Miami and Los Angeles if the same thing isn't happening to them. Make no mistake about it: What we have here is a land grab without an army, a mass migration across our borders so that they can have their same lives, unchanged, that they were living in Mexico. If new arrivals won't learn English and we tolerate it, then it's safe to say that eventually, we will all have to learn Spanish. That's all there is to it.

We Should Simply
Stop, Look And Listen!

When people refer to themselves as "Americans" they in effect are saying, "Yes, we may be from Hungary, the Philippines or Cuba, but we all share a common political ideal, an allegiance to one country, the United States of America and therefore are *one American people*. This is quite different from the second grouping of people who identify themselves as Hispanics or Latinos and say, "Yes, we may be from El Salvador, from Mexico, from Guatemala, but we all speak a common language, Spanish, and therefore are *one Latino people."*

When I look at the old film clips of people sailing into New York Harbor a century ago, they were all waving little American flags before they even set foot on American soil. From that point on, they always referred to their former homeland as "the old country" and gladly threw themselves into the blending that transformed all them into a new breed of human beings. In short, they became Americans.

Canada has always been about being this great patchwork of diversity and has supported bilingual education and other forms of the multi-cultural experience. Well, guess what? What began as an affirmation of diversity soon became an opening for separatists to get a foothold and sure enough, our worst nightmare has already occurred there. The Anglophones, those who speak English, are no longer comfortable in Montreal and are leaving the province as they feel like strangers in their own country. French is now the dominant language.

The Crux of the Problem

Many Hispanics feel entitled to the southern U.S. They do so pointing out that much of California and Texas were originally part of Mexico. While yes, this is true, it is also true that it was barren, undeveloped land before we came in and transformed it into what it has become today. The fact that many Mexicans in Mexico feel this way is scary enough. To then realize that the same view is held by Hispanics within our borders is even more frightening, given the fact that they now are the largest demographic group in California. It only goes to follow that, as the majority, they will one day want to force the state and possibly the nation to become bilingual.

Hispanics have already set up their little enclaves of Mexico right here in the US. This has created a situation where the people in Altoona, Pennsylvania or Miami, FL. or Los Angeles, CA. had better be prepared to speak Spanish when they go to the store or they may well return home empty handed.

I experienced this firsthand when I lived in Manhattan. There was a little "mom and pops store" directly across the street from my apartment building. I tried to get some essentials there once and found that none of the items had prices on them. When I asked how much for this or that, it became apparent that they didn't speak English so I couldn't buy anything. As I was leaving, I couldn't help but notice their total indifference at losing a sale.

It was clear that they felt it was purely my loss, not theirs. Over the years, they had developed a whole clientele of Spanish speaking people who had also become part of their insular little community and accordingly couldn't care less if I didn't shop there.

Is It Ethical to Deny Benefits?

It is once we recognize that nations are groupings of people, like families, or, if you like, condominium associations where individuals contribute to the whole with the assumption and reasonable expectation that the proceeds and subsequent benefits will not be dispensed to the world at large, or even to those who drop in, but rather will be reserved for those who by name and title are legally a part of that said union. Go ahead, try to find someone who can't understand that. A lot of people may not like it, but I'd venture to say that most, even if only privately, would accept this as an accurate and fair rendering of the issue at hand.

The Problem Is That We Have Turned The Whole Thing Completely Upside Down!

As impossibly backwards as it seems, most of us could accept this if the situation were reversed and we were the ones being denied benefits in a foreign land. Yet, when it comes to us standing up for ourselves and saying no to those who seek to draw from tax collected funds to which they have never contributed, we have a difficult time saying no. Why do we do this? How can we justify it? Remember: for something to be truly ethical, it must apply to a wide array of situations. In light of this, I remind us of the admonition to love our neighbors as ourselves.

Catch and Release
Is For Fishing
Not the Border Patrol

Why in the world would people stop crossing into the United States if the only penalty is a free flight home? The answer is being played out every day. They wouldn't! They just keep on coming back over and over again. How stupid can we be? As I see it, we can: (a) spend an infinite amount of money building a fence, that can be breached across hundreds and hundreds of miles, (b) continue to hand out free plane tickets home to the tune of millions of dollars a year, or (c) give ample warning, have it broadcast loud and clear and then have the Federal Government impose stiff five year sentences for those who cross into the country illegally. A small number may incur the sentence, but I doubt very many. It is a lot more humane and ethical than not having a strong deterrent and as a consequence continue to sit by and watch people die from trying to cross such an unforgiving terrain.

The Canadian
Guest Worker Program

It works because it is based on common sense. If Mexicans want to bypass the mess we have created for seasonal workers here in the US, they can contact Canadian authorities stationed in Mexico who, in turn, are able to match them with specific employers in Canada. Upon agreeing to the terms of their employment, these guest workers are given a plane ticket with the firm expectation that upon arrival they are to report directly to their employer, work at the agreed upon task and then, upon completion of the task, use the return portion of their ticket for their flight home. A failure by the worker or the employer to live up to their end of the bargain results in disqualification.

This is currently is in place in Canada as outlined in a lengthy segment broadcast on National Public Radio. When interviewed, both the workers and their employers stated that they loved it. When the program then went on to ask American officials their reaction to it, they were the ones who uttered disapproval. Why? Because they said it denied workers the flexibility to seek out a better situation if it didn't work out well with their employer. My response to this is that (1) even though it was not spelled out in the segment, I'm sure they have a grievance/mediation process in place precisely for such situations and (2) even if they don't, we must remember that this is only for a season.

I'm also sure employers are well aware that word circles quickly among workers as to who is and isn't a good employer and they don't want to be in the latter category as the next time around they don't want to go without a sufficient number of workers or be supplied with only the ones no one else will hire.

A Simple Plan
Our Policy Makers
Reject

Why? What is their reason? It denies workers their rights to shop around for something better once they arrive in the host country. Are they serious! If we open the door to our homes to folks we have never met before, we don't let them meander through the house and do as they please. No, if they have come to fix the water heater or paint the hallway or even use the bathroom, we either lead them to it or give them directions as to its location. But we don't stop there, we keep tabs on where they are until they leave. It's only logical!

There we have it. Here we are wondering why so may now enter our country and then blend into the scenery in L.A. or Miami, never to be seen again until they either seek permanent residency status or a green card, need medical care or get arrested. This is the reason. We throw open the doors and don't have in place a way of verifying their whereabouts once they get here. The ugly truth of the matter is that if it were not for political parties, we wouldn't be discussing immigrants outnumbering our citizens.

Instead, we'd be voting to cut off benefits and deny them work. Yet, the parties are resistant as it seems they value their own survival more than our survival as a nation.

Who Said Anything about Using Gestapo Like Round-ups Tactics?

Don't fall for the lies and terrible accusations of those wanting to ignore the integrity of our borders. They are quick to assert that the only way to get all of these people back to their home country is to resort to Gestapo like tactics complete with the mass rounding up of civilians, internment camps and other brutal measures similar to those used during World War II and earlier in history during the Veil of Tears. Talk about cheap shots! I find such ludicrous allegations to be as hate filled as they are utterly ridiculous. If we were such cruel and callous people, why would anyone even consider moving here in the first place? It's illogical.

Once we stop benefits to illegal recipients and actively work to improve living and working conditions in Mexico, they will start to migrate southward to their home country. This is not unfair. It is far more charitable and humane than many, if not most, countries would do under these circumstances. Again, if we were in another nation's borders illegally, there isn't a person among us who would find fault with us not getting benefits that were only intended for the pool of people who paid into their system. So, why is this any different when we are the country in question?

America, don't you dare cave in on this one! It is your country, dog gone it! Don't fall for the cheap guilt trips laid upon you by usurpers who have no legitimate right to be here. Their claim is as ridiculous as Indians showing up in Manhattan with a receipt and the trinkets used in the original transaction hoping we will give them the island. If this makes sense, why not just give the whole thing back to the Vikings?

People who have taken it upon themselves to either sneak in or stayed past their scheduled date of departure are the ones who should feel guilty, not us. They have no more right to our country than a passerby has the right to the keys to our homes or the money in our pensions.

Do whatever it takes to "preserve, protect and defend" not only the Constitution, but our country, "from all threats, both foreign and domestic." Rise up and vote out of office those candidates who would partial out this land incrementally neighborhood by neighborhood, city by city and state by state to those who wish to come here and set up offsite outposts of their native homelands. This country is not for sale and most certainly is not to be given away. The door is open, but it is only open to people who are willing to surrender any and all ties to former nations in order to pick up their new, all-consuming identity as Americans.

US Protects Every Border Except Ours?

There must have been a typo somewhere along the line for the US Military has somehow become the UN's Military. Now, a border incursion anywhere in the world sets off an immediate call for our deployment. This is not done lightly, however, as we won't act without first forming a "coalition of the willing" ... as in a long list of nations more than willing to let us do all of the heavy lifting. Yes indeed, thanks to our tax dollars, people the world over go to bed feeling secure ... unless, of course, they live in Arizona, Texas, California or Florida. For our troops are stationed to provide maximum protection for any international border except, of course, our very own. How do we justify this?

Isn't It Odd?

We don't fault Australia for denying entrance to anyone and everyone who can't pay huge amounts of money to move there, but we beat ourselves up for seeking to stem the flow of penniless immigrants who now number in the millions in California. Why such a cruel, self-hating double standard?

Three Questions
for Consideration

1) What would Canada look like without the Province of Quebec? Why do I ask? It's because it almost happened not too many years ago. It's true. They had a very close election and it may come up for a vote again.

2) What would Great Britain look like without Ireland? Why do I ask? It's because it almost happened within the past year. It, too, was a real squeaker of an election and could have gone either way with Ireland becoming independent.

3) What would the United States look like without California? Why do I ask? I don't know, other than to remind us that maps are redrawn all of the time. Just as Canada would have been severely be crippled if Quebec had just a few more votes in favor of succession and Great Britain would be forever diminished if the vote in Ireland had gone the other way, so, too, I shudder to think what this country would look like without its West Coast.

Any nation that allows foreigners to outnumber its own citizens is doing nothing short of creating the perfect environment for a revolt in either the voting booth or on the field of battle.

Do we really have to wait until there is an actual ballot initiative for secession similar to those in Canada and Great Britain before we realize how potentially dangerous it might be to just hand over a majority vote to a people who have never expressed an affinity for the country as a whole?

What About Our Government's Promises to its Own Citizens?

It's only ethical that the Federal Government honors its original promise to its own people before making any more. Before we look at this government's request to grant a blanket across the board amnesty to those living here illegally, let's look at the first time it asked for the same thing in 1986. I remember it clearly, but for those who don't, let's haul out the newspaper and television news accounts of that period. Do this and we'll see that this country has been more than generous. It went to ridiculous lengths to make sure every illegal alien had the opportunity to become full fledged American citizens with one caveat, that this offer would never be repeated again. That was the promise, the sales pitch, and on the basis of this promise, votes were cast.

Now, here we are 28 years later and we're back to square one. The only difference is that back then there were 3 million illegal residents in question. Today the number has swelled to four times that amount. Yet, the President and Congress assure us this will solve the problem of illegal immigration. Why on Earth would they think that? Better still, why on Earth would we believe them now?

It raises for me the question, "What right does the government have to violate its promise to its people?" It also leads me to suggest that if the original agreement was unfair or faulty, then fine, let's go back and revoke it. We'll just pretend that it never happened and retroactively nullify every citizenship paper that was issued under that agreement. Not fair? Why not? They can't have it both ways.

Two Parables

Once upon a time...

there lived two neighboring families. One had created a nice life for themselves. Everything had its place and was in order. As a result, their home became the envy of the neighborhood.

Immediately next door, life was not so good. It seemed that they lived in a constant state of disarray. Doors were left open, the lawn was never kept up and mowed, the children lacked discipline and the drama encircling their lives never seemed to wane. The contrast between the two neighbors could not have been more obvious.

It was only a matter of time before the children from the house of disarray started spending more and more time next door. They enjoyed all the niceties life at home failed to afford them and so it only made sense that they gravitated in their neighbor's direction. After all, it was a quick fix. All they had to do was travel the short distance and suddenly their lives dramatically improved to the extent that they never wanted to go home.

For a while this arrangement was acceptable, but in time two things were noticed. First, it didn't improve anything in the house of disarray, the source of their discontentment. Secondly, it was only a matter of time before their way of living impacted their neighbor's. Soon they were dealing with behaviors their guests brought with them and now instead of one house in disarray, there were two. The solution was not for the one family to walk away from their situation, but rather to address it and correct it there.

Again, once upon another time...

there lived a gentle giant. Its strength was unequalled and nothing could escape the length of its grasp. All of its neighbors came to rely on its strength and gentle benevolence as it had a special place in its heart for the weak, the defenseless and those in need of assistance.

In time, however, lesser forces around it came to realize that even a giant is itself vulnerable for giants tend to have giant hearts. Get to that heart, cause it to question its motivations and become inwardly conflicted and soon it will lose its strength of confidence.

That giant is not at all unlike the United States. It, too, needs a word of encouragement now and then, for no nation has had a bigger heart and gentle giants like this one are few and far between.

Will California Become Another Crimea?

Consider Crimea. Here we have a situation where people within Ukraine's borders had a deeper love for the neighboring country than they did for the land where they lived. In time, they voted to be annexed into that neighboring country. What's to keep the same thing from happening in this situation with Hispanics within our borders? Or again, as the new majority, why wouldn't they insist on the adoption of their native tongue, Spanish, in all aspects of life including all speeches in the halls of Congress and the printing of bilingual currency?

The question then transitions to that of why? Why would we freely give away our homeland to a foreign people who, unless they are abnormally different from every other grouping of people, would naturally move to secure this land as theirs and alter its institutions to reflect them, thereby making us feel like foreigners in our own land? Why? Why? Why?

Logic Itself Calls Us
To Consider The Following:

1) Given that these immigrants have persisted in keeping Spanish as their primary language when they had no power, what leads us to believe they will start speaking English once we give Hispanics a majority vote in California by making them US citizens?

2) Again, haven't we been watching the news? Nation after nation is being divided along linguistic lines. Do we really want to run the risk of becoming yet one more country to reaffirm a great truth uttered by none other than Jesus Christ who warned that "a house divided cannot stand?"

3) If we couldn't keep the door closed and secure California's border when Americans were in the majority, what on earth makes us think the door won't be opened even wider with a Mexican majority that will naturally want to have their families join them?

4) Minors should assume the same legal status as their parents. If the parent is an illegal resident,

then the child is an illegal resident. This only makes sense.

Fix the problems where they are, in Mexico. Flee from them and they will surely follow.

We Do Need to Be the Very Best of Neighbors.

Mexico is a mess and our addiction to drugs is not solely, but largely, responsible. The solution is not for Mexicans to flee north as that will only worsen things there and go on to create a myriad of problems here.

Let's stop encouraging far flung people to walk away the challenges they face. Instead, let's assist them in finding real solutions. We need to redirect aid from hostile nations and send those funds to help our neighbors to the south. For we really do need to pitch in and do our part, but we need to do it in such a way that really and truly helps Mexico while at the same time honoring the vision of our nation, namely that we remain a melting pot, not a collection of separate people!

We Should Affirm
Our National Motto:
E Pluribus Unum
(Out Of Many One)

We should ponder, meditate on, take stock of and live up to our National Motto: E pluribus Unum".....Out of Many One. It is a powerful statement, a vision our founding fathers (and mothers) had for this country and a sobering acknowledgement of the simple fact that in order to pick up and fully embrace something new, a relinquishing, putting down and walking away from things previously cherished must first take place. It is akin to the vows in a wedding ceremony where all else takes a back seat to the supremacy of a love between two people.

This theme is not only verbalized, but literally acted out in the actual staging of the ceremony which, like a play, opens with the bride being escorted in by her father. His presence represents her family and her life up to that point. It affirms the past and yet there is a poignant moment when he stops and withdraws once the bride reaches the front of the sanctuary and joins her future husband. Yet, she is not the only one called upon to leave the past behind and make sacrifices as during the ceremony the groom is also admonished to leave his father and mother and cleave only to his wife.

Once the couple is positioned together, standing side by side, this theme of separating, of pulling away from all other concerns is advanced again, this time by the congregation who is asked if they know of any previously held allegiances or any "just cause" why these two cannot be joined together. This settled, the couple is then bid to move even further ahead in their shared path of exclusion, this time away from even their closest friends, their maids of honor and groomsmen until they finally arrive at the altar. It is there that they alone, in a very intimate, but public moment, take solemn vows and declare to the world that through thick and thin, good times and bad, they are in it until death do they part.

Then and only then are they spun around and reintroduced to their friends and family as if for the very first time. They are now a new reality, a new family unit with a new name and identity, ready to face the blessings and challenges that lie before them.

Emboldened with a joy rooted in confidence, they do not walk; they do not mosey or saunter, nor prance or dance. To the contrary, they boldly march, arm in arm to the triumphant strains of "the wedding march" right through the middle of the crowd stopping for no one or no thing and keep right on going out the doors of the church and into the glistening reality of the new life they have established together.

Against this backdrop, I look at the illegal immigrants who have arrived here in our midst unannounced and uninvited. They say they seek the blessings of a new relationship, but have been unyielding in their utter determination to surrender nothing and remain the same as before they broke our laws by crossing our borders. They want to keep their "proud Hispanic heritage," their way of life, their language, even their right to continue voting in Mexican (as well as) American elections. Each one of these actions on their part only reaffirms the obvious fact that they don't want to have anything to do with becoming part of our grand union. Having heard and witnessed their endlessly reaffirmed deep down decision to remain unchanged, we need only feel entirely comfortable in saying to them with equal clarity of voice, "Adios and Good bye."

My Take on the Presidency

A great President is one who is able to see things far enough ahead to steer this massive ship of state away from the rocks and into deep majestic waters where it can stretch its legs. It's about seeing the much bigger picture and sharing the vision, then taking decisive steps to achieve it while at the same time exuding the joy and confidence that bespeaks the best of what this nation has to offer.

We live in troubling times, when the great visionaries of the age have either gone on before us or all but lost their voices. Yet, I am confident that the same hope that has seen us through tougher times will see us through yet again. It is alive and well in the American classroom where children are still taught that justice is not expendable and virtue has a price. It is the promise of the living uttered at memorials to fallen heroes that their sacrifice will not only be remembered, but held high as an inspiration so that when our time comes, we will not falter.

Since Lincoln, no incoming President has had the challenge of healing the wounds of such a deeply divided land. Indeed, it is this division, this inner turmoil and angst that threatens to render us powerless against the challenges we would otherwise find so infinitely surmountable.

As a good and noble people, we are quick to evaluate and judge ourselves by standards we would immediately feel harsh in applying to others. This has caused us to sink into the phantom pain of misplaced guilt that lesser nations have placed upon us in an attempt to dodge their own much needed introspection.

I take up the challenge their brooding thoughts illicit. Let me, as an ever proud American, tell you about this country and its people. It is, to the very best of my knowledge, the only nation in recorded history that routinely rebuilds the countries that have savagely waged war against it. Am I wrong? What other nation, either today or in history, has ever done so. I very much doubt one can be named.

Then, there is the shame that should be upon us for the awful names we have called our enemies in the heat of battle. We have called the Japanese "Japs", the Germans "Gerry's" and communists "commies." How terrible, abbreviating their names like that. Why, it is every bit as bad as calling the folks in Oklahoma "Okies!" Shame on us.

Name a nation that is as reluctant as this republic to go into battle, and when it does so is almost always there solely to lend support to a nation under siege. Take Viet Nam, the birthplace of much of this inner self-loathing, as an example. History bears witness to the simple fact that we had nothing whatsoever to gain in that conflict. We reluctantly went in for purely humanitarian reasons as there weren't any economic or territorial incentives to be gained. We went in for one reason and one reason only, namely to support the South Vietnamese who were under attack from communist forces.

The same defensive role was taken by us in the previous decade on the Korean Peninsula, when once again, communist forces in the north attacked the democratic forces in the south. In both conflicts, the United States was simply trying to stop the real, not merely perceived, but real spread of global communism. Had the US elected not to do so, it would not itself have suffered as it was more than able to defend itself from any real or perceived threat in that era.

Indeed, the US could have returned to the comfortable quiet life of the Eisenhower years, but didn't. Instead, it stood up for vulnerable South

Vietnam against the onslaught of the North even though it did long term damage to our own sense of who we are and what we are about.

We forget that in August of 1961, the communists put up the Berlin Wall. Only fourteen short months later, in October of 1962, we had the Cuban Missile Crisis. These events took place at the very same time that Soviet Premier Nikita Khrushchev was verbally haranguing the United Nations with his support of taking these aggressive measures global.

To recap, there were aggressive acts on the part of communists in the Western Hemisphere (Cuba), in Europe (Berlin) and in Southeast Asia (Vietnam). The only force positioned to stop them was the United States. Given that the communists did prevail in Cuba and Berlin, I certainly understand our refusal to stand idly by and watch them prevail in Vietnam. I, for one, am grateful to those who fought for the defense of individual freedom in that land. We may have lost that battle, but I'm wise enough to know that the larger war, the war for the right to self-determination, is far from over. There's no doubt in my mind that without the extreme sacrifice of those who fought, suffered and died, other incursions would have taken place.

Enough said. I am not in denial about our shortcomings. This book speaks volumes about our flirtation with greed and the recent loss of our moral compass. At the same time, however, I will probably be the very last person to ever give up on us. And even if, God forbid, we do not now find permission within to pick ourselves up off the mat and fight for our nation, my hope and prayer is that we will at least rise up in defense of a troubled world that would sorely miss the most generous, self-effacing ally it has ever had. With this in mind, I, with all that is within, pray that God will continue to direct, forgive, ennoble and bless this mighty land.

Two Notions Politicians Routinely Peddle:

1) *They're nobler than the rest because, unlike their counterparts, they're the ones who are "working within the system for change."*

2) *Accordingly, from time to time, they have no choice but to make compromises. They do so reluctantly, however, as part and parcel of the on-going heavy price they routinely suffer to advance the nobler causes they were sent to Washington to address.*

This pretty much covers it, doesn't it?

If folks like what they do and how they vote, then that's wonderful. If voters don't approve, that's still OK because politicians can always claim they had to do it to stay in place for future battles.

It's a bit like having a police force, or better yet, a military that proudly boasts it will do whatever it takes to protect the country just as long as its soldiers are never in harm's way. And why is that? We are told it is because the generals have to ensure the safety of their soldiers in order to keep them for our protection in the future...just as long as, like today's encounters with the enemy...they remain completely safe and free from danger.

This line of thinking is eerily similar to today's professional, career politicians. They suffer from a collective delusion of grandeur, the deep seated belief in their own political indispensability which in turn has led to the erroneous notion that we cannot possibly make it without them. Once this thought is firmly entrenched in their minds and hearts, we see that everything is negotiable when it comes to keeping themselves and their political party in power.

Final Thoughts on Forming
a More Perfect Union

I want more than anything for us to continue on as a democracy, but in order to do so, we have to dump this dysfunctional way of doing things. Quite simply, if the only way we can get beyond our inner desire to take up sides against each other is to have our government fund athletic teams, then let's do it. That is more than fine with me, but for goodness' sake, let's get this mentality of competing out of our heads when it comes to drafting legislation. For in the final analysis, it shouldn't boil down to winners versus losers. It should come down to knowing beyond any reasonable doubt that we as a people have come as close as possible to making clean, well thought out choices.

Again, the crux of the problem is the process. I am convinced that once we stand far enough back from it to see just how self-defeating it has become, we'll hopefully see through this ridiculous practice of dividing ourselves up, going to opposite ends of the field and commencing to run headlong into each other at full tilt only to later question why, all stymied and bloody, we don't get farther.

No wonder other nations are pulling ahead. It's as though we have somehow convinced ourselves that we must always dwell in a scaled back version of the Civil War, except of course, and on those rare dates like December 8, 1941 or September 12, 2001, the days immediately after we were savagely attacked. At least on those days we were one people, united together, waving American flags and singing God Bless America instead of squaring off in opposing camps.

The haunting image I have in my mind's eye of the United States' situation today is that we are tragically like a football stadium filled with spectators who are so caught up in the competition on the field that they fail to pay adequate attention to the fact that just outside the arena, opponents, in this case the Chinese, have surrounded the entire complex and are positioning themselves to move in for the kill.

Clearly, our political process has become too inwardly focused, too energy absorbing and too distracting to meet the needs of a 21st century nation that must immediately pull out of its nose dive if it is to have any hope of surviving.

Why don't we keep the free speech, keep the frank dialoging, keep the decision making of the people, for the people and by the people and then go the next step and dump the whole notion of putting ourselves on teams. For as long as we have teams, be they Republicans and Democrats, or what-have-you versus what-have- you, we will by definition be a nation divided. Why not only have only one team and as one team only have one adversary, evil? Hey, it worked for the writers of Superman, you know, "truth, justice and the American way." It all makes sense to me.

If only we could do this, I think we'd make old Benjamin Franklin, George Washington, Thomas Jefferson and the whole gang back in 1776 all the more proud. For then we will have reclaimed the essence of what they were about. It's not the influence of money or power or prestige, nor is it about getting one's way. To the contrary, it is about emptying ourselves of our own interests that people in power might hear and lend voice to the average citizen. After all, the quest of the American Revolution was to form a government so reflective of the people it served that its members were not given titles consistent with royalty, but rather the more humble title of a House of Representatives.

LIST OF HEADINGS

www.ingramcontent.com/pod-product-compliance
Lightning Source LLC
Chambersburg PA
CBHW070927290526
45795CB00001B/458